INTRODUCTION

Parents and family have the greatest impact on young children's attitudes, values, and behavior. As a parent, you are your child's best teacher, and the responsibility of modeling responsible behavior is yours. Nurturing a sense of responsibility now, when your child is young, can make a lasting difference in his or her life.

Although responsibility means different things to different people, a true sense of responsibility means that we are motivated from the inside to follow rules that help us and help others. Help your child become aware that there are many rules that both adults and children must follow to maintain healthy relationships with their family, their community, and their world.

Because children learn by doing, the way to teach them responsibility is to give them daily opportunities to be responsible. *Raising Responsible Kids* is filled with activities that are designed to help you nurture your child's inner sense of responsibility, one that is motivated not so much by obedience, but by your child's own desire to be responsible. Use the ideas in this book to teach your child about responsible behavior every day, in many simple, age-appropriate ways that are a part of ordinary family life.

A Word About Safety: The activities in *Raising Responsible Kids* are appropriate for young children between the ages of 3 and 5. However, keep in mind that if a project calls for using small objects, an adult should supervise at all times to make sure that children do not put the objects in their mouths. It is recommended that you use art materials that are specifically labeled as safe for children unless the materials are to be used only by an adult.

CONTENTS

Cultivating Self-Discipline	2
Nurturing a Work Ethic	6
Nurturing Family Responsibility	10
Dealing with Family Challenges	14
Nurturing Community Responsibility	18
Introducing Social Skills	22
Nurturing Anti-Bias Attitudes	26
Cultivating Environmental Awareness	30

Brighter Vision Publications   BV15022 Raising Responsible Kids

Cultivating Self-Discipline

Making Rules and Setting Limits

Children feel secure when they know what is expected of them.

Being self-aware enough to know what you can and cannot do is a sign of self-discipline. One of the best ways to begin to help your child understand what behaviors are permissible in your home is to make a few simple rules that address these limitations.

When you make rules, word them so that they reflect the behaviors that you want to encourage in your child. For example, if you want your child to stop making sculptures on your kitchen floor, you might make the following rule: "We play with modeling dough only on this table." Another rule might be "Talk very softly when baby is sleeping" or "All preschoolers in our home must take a nap after lunch." Let your child help you make family rules, and discuss why the rules are important and how they help us. When you remind your child about a rule, ask him to think and remember what the rule is about.

Cultivating Self-Discipline

Making Choices

Give your child the chance to practice decision making every day.

If you want your child to learn about self-discipline and responsibility, it's very important to give her the experience of making choices. Structure these choices so that they are appropriate for the age of your child. For example, as the parent, you must decide which breakfast cereals are healthy for your child. But you could keep a few different brands of healthy cereal on hand and let your child choose each day which one she wants. Your child can also make choices about which bedtime story to read, which toys to clean up first, or which of several outfits to wear. The older your child gets, the more choices you can make available to her.

However, don't offer your child a choice if there really is no choice. For example, if you want her to pick up her toys and get ready for bed, don't ask, "Would you like to stop playing now? Isn't it time for bed soon?" Instead, say, "In about five minutes you will need to pick up your toys and start getting ready for bed." When five minutes are up, tell her, "Now it's time to pick up. Are you going to pick up the blocks first or the cars first?"

Time-Out

Encourage your child to visualize positive behavior.

A time-out is a disciplinary method that can be used to teach self-control. Giving your child a time-out means removing her from the scene of misbehavior. When you give your child a time-out, try to avoid shaming her or becoming emotional. Set up a chair for her to sit in quietly in a place without distractions such as a corner or hallway, and don't let her leave the chair until the time-out is over. Try to keep the duration of the time-out short and consistent; two to three minutes is all that is necessary for young children. Placing an hourglass or an alarm clock near your child during her time-out, so that she can keep track of the time, may make the discipline more bearable.

Time-outs are most effective if your child understands and can tell you what she did that was inappropriate. Explain that she needs to take time to think about a different and better way to behave. Encourage her to use the time to calm down, regain self-control, and decide she is ready to follow the rules.

When the time-out is over, there is no need to express anger or to dwell on her misbehavior. Ask her if she is ready to behave now. Then hug her and give her a chance to start over.

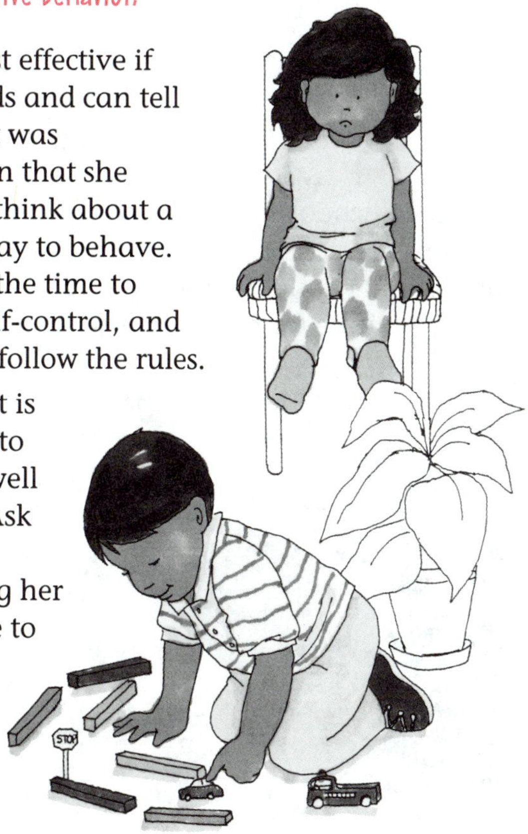

Cultivating Self-Discipline

Calming Down and Taking Breaks

To stay balanced and emotionally fit, everyone needs a natural rhythm in their daily activities.

Young children need to be taught how to calm themselves down periodically during their day. If your child seems unusually loud or rowdy, it may be a sign that he is overexcited or overtired. Try to become aware of these signs in your child and teach him to recognize for himself when he is losing control, becoming too loud, or moving too fast. Set clear rules or expectations for your child's play, and encourage him to take breaks often. Help him learn to pace himself by developing a special signal for break time, or by stepping in occasionally to ask if he thinks he could use a break to catch his breath and play more cooperatively. Here are some good breaktime strategies.

- Talking quietly together
- Napping
- Snacking
- Looking at books
- Drawing
- Slow-motion activities such as pantomiming and moon walking
- Deep breathing
- Gentle exercising (bending and stretching)

When he can stop on his own and take a "calm down" break, he is truly accepting responsibility for his well-being.

Bedtimes

Always prepare children ahead of time for the end of their day.

Your preschooler needs between 8 and 11 hours of sleep each night, with consistent bedtime routines and regular bedtime hours. If you set up a simple routine for him to follow, your child is old enough to get ready for bed by himself. His bedtime routine should be a calm, relaxed time of about 30 minutes. It might include a shared time when you eat a snack together, talk quietly, read a bedtime story, and tuck him in for the night. It might also include time for toileting, putting dirty clothes away, washing face and hands, and brushing teeth. Coach your child to learn this routine with your cues. "It will be time to put your pajamas on in ten minutes." Later, "Now it's time to brush your teeth." When children practice a consistent nightly routine, they feel secure and more relaxed. They also learn the discipline they'll need to get ready for bed independently.

Cultivating Self-Discipline

Getting Dressed

Your child will feel grown up if he has some control over what he wears.

Make the process of dressing and undressing easy for your child by selecting pullover sweaters and jackets, sweatpants and sweatshirts without drawstrings, elastic-waist pants, and slip-on shoes or shoes with Velcro closures. Involve your child in choosing what to wear each day, dressing himself, and taking care of the clothes he takes off. Here are some other ways to help your child become more responsible for his clothing.

- Give your child a hamper, a basket, a tote bag, or an old pillowcase with his name written on it to put his daily dirty clothes in.
- Let your child help you fold his clothes and put them away in his dresser or clothes closet.
- Make a shoe storage area out of crates or shoeboxes.
- Hang clothes hangers and hooks in your child's room so that they are easy for him to reach.
- Practice using buttons, zippers, and snaps by draping adult-size jackets or sweaters over the back of a chair.

Mealtimes

Family-style meals offer opportunities for good manners and conversation.

Preschoolers know how to feed themselves, so they can now take on additional responsibilities at meals. Instead of filling your child's plate, let her serve herself.

If you serve meals buffet style, make it easy for her by setting the food out on low tables. Cut portions of each food into small pieces that are easier for her to put on her plate, and include teaspoons along with larger serving spoons. Fill a plastic measuring cup with water, milk, or juice, and let your child use it as a pitcher so she can pour her own drink. Slice butter into pats, or set out tubs of soft butter or margarine so your child can butter her own roll or bread, and put condiments in squeeze containers or in small bowls so she can choose her own independently. If you pass the food around the table "family style," use small, lightweight serving bowls and refill them often. Seat your child near the end of the passing line so the portions aren't too heavy for her to lift. If the meat is difficult to cut or if she hasn't mastered this skill yet, cut it for her ahead of time and place it on the platter. Say "please" and "thank you" when you are passing food around and set simple family guidelines about clearing the table so that everyone, including your child, is involved.

Brighter Vision Publications — BV15022 Raising Responsible Kids

Nurturing a Work Ethic

Mommy's and Daddy's Jobs

Being part of the family team means that parents often must work outside the home.

Children soon learn that their parents' jobs are connected to money, and that money is exchanged to get items that the family needs or wants. Working outside the home is often necessary and is one of the most important things that parents do to cooperate as part of the family team.

To help your child begin to understand your job, arrange to take him to your workplace for a visit. Let him see where you work, observe what you do there, and meet other people you work with. Your child will learn that in your job you cooperate with other people every day. He will see that everyone works together to get things done.

If your child cannot visit your workplace, take photos to show him and talk about later. Knowing more about your job may also ease his anxiety when you are away at work and help him to be more cooperative when you are gone.

If you are a stay-at-home dad or mom, make your child aware that everything you do around the house, from washing clothes to cooking meals, is part of your job.

Nurturing a Work Ethic

The Help-Out Habit

Give your child many opportunities to establish the habit of helping.

Encouraging your child to help out in small ways as a family member and to take pride in these responsibilities is the first step toward nurturing a positive work ethic. Provide your child with many opportunities for helping out around your house. If you show your appreciation for her contributions, your child will enjoy working with you, whether you ask her to fetch or carry, set the table, sort clean laundry, or scrub vegetables. Keep in mind that it is the habit of cooperating in this way that is important, not how perfectly she does her tasks.

The following are more ideas for jobs your preschooler can help you with.

- Taking care of pets
- Watering plants
- Washing the car
- Vacuuming the carpet
- Putting groceries away
- Dusting furniture
- Pulling weeds or bagging leaves
- Making lunch

The Allowance Debate

If handled effectively, a regular allowance can be a great teaching tool.

The topic of allowance raises a lot of questions. Should children be given an allowance? Is an allowance a right, or a privilege to be earned? At what age should children begin to receive an allowance?

Whether you decide to give your child an allowance is an individual family decision. When to begin giving your child an allowance is also up to you. If you think your child is old enough to have money, and if you are willing to help him take responsibility for the money that you give him, then you are ready to begin.

If you do decide to give him an allowance, think of it as a tool for teaching him about the value of money. Along with the money, introduce him to the concepts of spending, saving, and earning. Make behavior a separate issue from his allowance so that he won't link money with punishment or reward. If you decide to not give an allowance, consider giving your child money for small purchases when you go shopping. Or keep a change jar on hand for him to dip into with permission, so that he will have experiences in spending money.

Brighter Vision Publications

BV15022 Raising Responsible Kids

Nurturing a Work Ethic

Learning About Money

Help your child realize that money is a medium of exchange.

If you decide to give your child an allowance, take steps beforehand to prepare her for this privilege and responsibility. Help her understand the concept of money in terms of number and quantity by giving her the opportunity to use money in and out of your home.

At home, let your child sort and count real coins, and play pretend store with real coins. When you shop, let her help you buy items at the grocery such as cereal or fruit. Money games for children can be found in the books *A Penny Saved* and *Money Doesn't Grow on Trees* by Neale S. Godfrey.

Delayed Gratification

Teach your child the value of saving money to buy something special.

One of the hardest life lessons that your child needs to learn is that he cannot always have what he wants when he wants it. Don't rush out to buy your child the latest toy he asks for. Instead, consider teaching him about delayed gratification. Tell him that some things have to be earned, and it takes time to save up money to buy something special that you want. Give your child two containers or jars, one for money he can spend at any time, and one for money to be saved for buying something special or expensive. Encourage him to put at least a part of his money in the savings jar every week.

Help him set realistic goals about saving. If your child wants to buy a gerbil, for example, first talk with him about all of the other purchases he will need to make to keep the gerbil in your home. In two weeks, your child will probably not have saved enough money to buy a gerbil, but he may have enough to purchase gerbil food, or a wheel for it to exercise on. He may need to keep saving in order to get a gerbil cage, but he could purchase a gerbil water bottle in the meantime.

Nurturing a Work Ethic

Learning from Choices

Encourage your child to learn from her purchases.

One way to build a foundation for responsible money management is to let your child make her own spending choices with her disposable income. Try not to interfere as she spends her money, so that she has the opportunity to learn from her spending choices.

Perhaps your child will buy candy that looks good but doesn't taste good to her. If this happens, don't replace the money. Your child needs to accept the responsibility of poor choices and learn from these experiences. If you let your child make small mistakes with a little bit of money, chances are she won't repeat the same mistakes on a larger scale.

Family Savings Bank

Your child will learn that a goal is easier to achieve when everyone contributes.

With your family, decide on a special event you would like to attend or a short trip that you would like to take together. Then choose a piggy bank or an unusual container in which to save money for the outing. If you like, turn an empty plastic jug into a "piggy bank" by using permanent markers, glue, and scraps of felt to make eyes, ears, a nose, and other features. Then add a curled pipe-cleaner tail and a cut-out slit for depositing money.

Decide as a family how your pig will be "fed." For instance, you might all agree to feed it a certain amount from allowances or to empty loose change into it once a week. Or, you may decide that you will put any "found" money into it. Find ways for every child in the family to "earn" money to put in the bank. When it's time to take out the money, count it together and celebrate the family's teamwork.

Nurturing Family Responsibility

Belonging is Crucial

It's important to help your child feel connected to others.

Children are often uprooted from the ties they form with friends and communities because of divorce, separation, job relocation, or unemployment. For this reason, it's all the more important to give them a strong sense of belonging to your family. Children who feel a sense of belonging are less likely to have problems getting along with others as they mature. When children feel the security of roots in their families and communities, they are better able to understand the many ways they contribute to and benefit from them.

Here are a few ways to foster feelings of belonging.

- Enlist the help of your relatives to make a family tree.
- Volunteer for a local organization and take your child to its functions.
- Write to family members on a regular basis.
- Visit family members as often as possible.
- Establish family rituals that can be carried out regardless of where you live, such as having a sing-along during the holidays or taking a walk together on the first day of spring.
- Organize a neighborhood block party.

Brighter Vision Publications · BVI5022 Raising Responsible Kids

Nurturing Family Responsibility

Holding Family Meetings

Use communication to develop cooperation and group problem-solving skills.

Plan regular family meetings that include your child. During these meetings, take turns sharing things that you noticed and appreciated about one another's behavior as well as concerns that you feel should be aired. To emphasize cooperation and problem solving, make sure that each family member has a turn to speak and that everyone speaks calmly, politely, and candidly.

You might start your meetings by sharing positive things. Then get any complaints out into the open. Brainstorm as a team to make and/or change family rules. Use your family meetings to demonstrate honest communication, which is the basis of positive social relationships.

Family Manners

Remembering good manners is everyone's responsibility.

Using good manners is a responsible way to show respect for others. Make it a family habit to practice good manners every day. When parents get too busy or preoccupied to model good manners, young children drop this good habit very quickly.

If you notice that your child is forgetting to mind his manners, try this experiment. Set up a recorder and tape your conversation during a family meal. You may be surprised to find that you have fallen out of the habit of saying "please" and "thank you," too.

Brighter Vision Publications — BV15022 Raising Responsible Kids

Nurturing Family Responsibility

New Family Members

A new baby in the house provides many opportunities to take responsibility.

Your older child will enjoy doing many small things to help you care for your new baby. Including her in chores such as these will make her feel important and grown up.

- Fetching and carrying diapers
- Helping fold baby clothes
- Playing quietly when baby is sleeping
- Helping mix baby's rice cereal
- Helping feed baby
- Helping keep pets away from baby
- Helping sing baby to sleep
- Helping keep small toys away from baby's reach

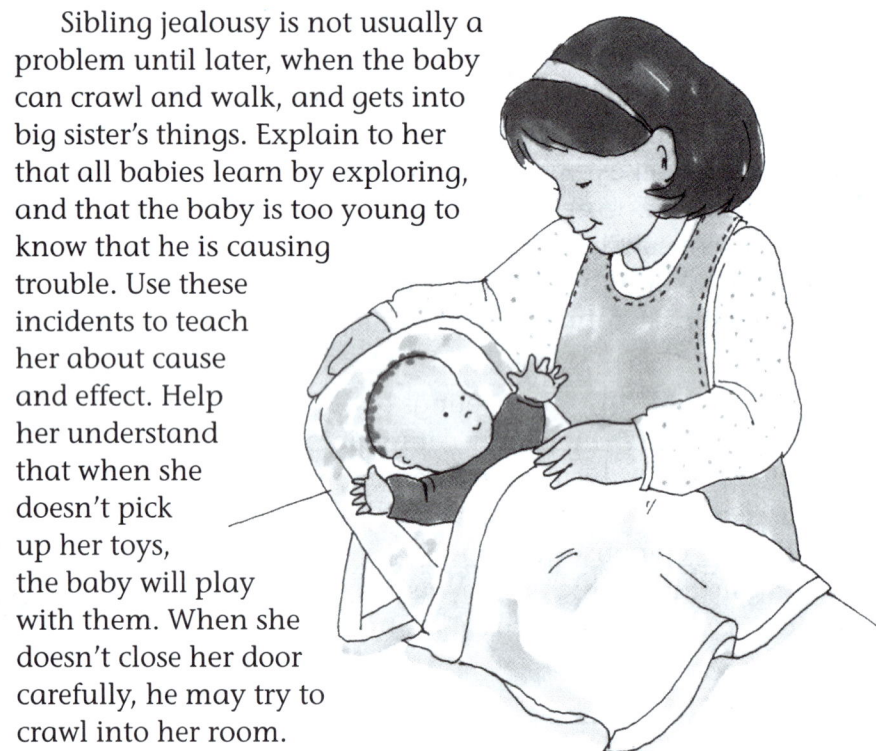

Sibling jealousy is not usually a problem until later, when the baby can crawl and walk, and gets into big sister's things. Explain to her that all babies learn by exploring, and that the baby is too young to know that he is causing trouble. Use these incidents to teach her about cause and effect. Help her understand that when she doesn't pick up her toys, the baby will play with them. When she doesn't close her door carefully, he may try to crawl into her room.

The Family Team

Family teamwork is your young child's first experience in group cooperation.

The family is not only a group of people who live together, it is a team in which all members cooperate to help make days run smoothly for everyone. Working together makes jobs easier and faster, so there is more time for family fun.

Help your child understand that cooperative teamwork is the fair way to do things. Show him that when everyone helps out, no one person has to do an unfair share of the work. For example, if each family member cooperates by clearing his or her own place after dinner, no one person has to clear the entire table. Or, if each person puts away his or her own dirty clothes, no one person has to spend the time collecting all the dirty laundry.

Nurturing Family Responsibility

Working with Grandparents

Don't overlook grandparents as a source of loving support for your child.

Supportive grandparents who live close by can usually be counted on to help out with their grandchildren, give advice, and generally be in the parents' corner through all family challenges. Whenever possible, encourage frequent visits and lots of communication between your child and your parents, and nurture common interests you see developing. If you are divorced, make sure that your child maintains a positive relationship with both sets of her grandparents.

When your ideas of parenting and the grandparents' ideas differ, try not to "sweat the small stuff." But hold firm on issues that you have strong feelings about and that involve your values. Grandparents need to understand that you are the parent, and your parental authority needs to be maintained for the emotional well-being of your child.

Distant Relatives

Remind your relatives that staying in touch is a mutual responsibility.

If your family is spread apart, your child may not feel connected to his extended family. He may only know or remember your distant relatives from family stories and photographs. Help strengthen these family ties by vacationing near family members, phoning regularly with your child, and arranging family reunions. Involve your child in these and other ideas for keeping in touch.

- Making short audio or video tapes
- Turning photos of your family into postcards
- Starting a family newsletter
- Sending "Thank-you" notes
- Sending greeting cards
- Beginning a story and sending it to a relative to add onto or complete
- Sending your child's paintings and drawings as gifts

Ask your distant relatives to send photos and notes to your child, and keep these items in a family scrapbook. Before visiting them, encourage them to send pictures of their house, their family, their pets, and their neighborhood to your child. These pictures will help you prepare your child for the visit and spark familiar memories when you arrive.

Brighter Vision Publications

BV15022 Raising Responsible Kids

Dealing with Family Challenges

Handling Sibling Rivalry

There are ways to help when your children don't get along.

Young children learn a great deal about being themselves and interacting with others from the challenges of living with brothers and sisters. When they share with one another, they learn how to cooperate and compromise, even though they may do a lot of arguing in the process. If sibling rivalry is one of your family challenges, here are some tips that may reduce the arguing and stress.

- Whenever possible, use humor to break the tension and then help your children use problem-solving skills to reach solutions on their own.
- Encourage teamwork in many ways, including setting family goals together and fostering open communication at family meetings.
- Diffuse rivalry and strengthen teamwork by not taking sides. Encourage your children to take responsibility for resolving differences.
- Give each child time alone with you so that you can observe and nurture individual strengths. Encourage each child's own interests and friendships to help your children focus on what they are able to do separately as well as together.
- Keep in mind that not all brothers and sisters are close when they are growing up, often because of personality differences. If this is the case in your family, accept these differences and respect them.
- Think of your home as a practice ground for life instead of a battleground for personalities.

Brighter Vision Publications

BV15022 Raising Responsible Kids

Dealing with Family Challenges

Family Adversities

Cooperation and support are vital when families go through tough times.

Sharing the difficult times in your family's life is just as important as sharing the fun and good times. By hiding problems from their young children, parents prevent them from taking responsibility as cooperative, supportive team members.

The best way to help your child cope with a family crisis is to give him honest, accurate information, explaining the problem simply in words that he can understand. When children don't know the whole story, what they imagine can be more frightening and confusing than the truth. Truth, clearly stated, gives children more freedom to be supportive and caring.

Too Bossy

Help a child with a bossy streak improve her behavior.

Children who are bossy often have potentially good leadership skills, but they need to learn how to soften their approach and become more sensitive toward others. They may need to play with a broader mix of children, including older children who are less likely to tolerate being bossed, and children who exhibit bossy streaks themselves. If you have a child who tends to be bossy, here are some suggestions.

- Help her develop interests through which she can meet friends.
- Encourage her potential for generosity and her ways of caring for others.
- When she is engaged in pretend play with friends, if she seems to be "directing the whole show," tactfully join in the play to involve her friends.
- When friends come over, remind her that they are guests and that they should be asked what kinds of play activities they prefer.
- If she is an only child who has difficulty with cooperation and other social skills, consider joining or forming a play group with families of other only children.
- Become involved in youth outreach or student exchange programs that will put her in touch with positive, older role models.

Dealing With Family Challenges

Tattling

Teach your child to put her observation skills to work for your family instead of against it.

Tattling is a bad habit that disrupts family harmony. It can reward your child with lots of negative attention, the thrill of making you lose your temper, and the satisfaction of getting what she wants. Nip this habit in the bud by convincing your child that she will get more attention from you if she "tattles" about the positive things she sees.

The next time your child tattles, admire her observation skills. Tell her that some people such as reporters and scientists have jobs that depend on being good observers and sharing what they observe with others. Invite your child to pretend to be a reporter or scientist and observe your family. Ask her to find three good things to say about one of the members of your family.

Helping Special Needs Children

Children need to learn that they can cope by experiencing and resolving problems.

Overprotecting special-needs children makes it much harder for them to learn independence, life skills, and cooperation with others. All children need to learn that sometimes we cannot do things others can, but we can do our personal best. They also need to learn that sometimes friends are unkind, and that it can be hard to cooperate, especially if we think that people don't like us.

Use the same guidelines and clear expectations for a child with special needs as you would for other children. Provide consistent family routines, orderly and well-organized personal space, time for active physical play, and daily opportunities to use open-ended art materials and engage in creative activities.

Avoid making excuses or exceptions for any uncooperative or inappropriate behavior. Most important, find ways that your challenged child can help someone else who is less fortunate in some way. Ask your church leader, your doctor, your child-care director, or your volunteer center for ideas about how to accomplish this.

Brighter Vision Publications

BVI5022 Raising Responsible Kids

Dealing with Family Challenges

Divorce

Parents who are no longer together can still help their child learn about cooperation and caring.

If you are a parent who is divorced or separated and are communicating with your former spouse, it is especially important that the two of you model cooperation for your child.

At times, you may need to discuss differences privately, but make sure that you always maintain positive language, behavior, and cooperation in all matters that relate to her. She loves both of you and wants the two of you to be friends, even if you are not together.

Your child is adjusting to many changes in the family situation and needs the security that your positive interactions will provide.

Try to not make a fuss about "picky" things regarding visiting arrangements. Of course, safety is always important. But it really doesn't matter if she sleeps in a sleeping bag for a night or two or skips eating salad or vegetables for a day.

The important thing is that your child is spending special time with someone she loves.

Overactive Children

Trust your own observations and instincts when deciding what is normal behavior for your child.

Most preschoolers learn through active, hands-on play. It's important to understand the stages of early childhood development so that you don't label energetic children as hyperactive or overactive when they are really just being normal.

Hyperactivity can only be diagnosed and treated by qualified and experienced professionals. Try not to let the opinions of relatives, teachers, or other parents influence you unless you have made a similar assessment of your child's behavior and activity levels. If you are really concerned about hyperactivity, ask for a free diagnostic exam through your physician or your school district's early childhood/preschool special education department. If your child does have a problem, treatment will help him learn to manage his behavior and act with more self-restraint and self-discipline.

Brighter Vision Publications

BVI5022 Raising Responsible Kids

Nurturing Community Responsibility

Respecting the Property of Others

Teach your child to be as careful with the belongings of others as she is with her own.

Children understand what it means to own something. Their belongings are intensely important to them. What they need to learn is that others feel the same way about the things that they own. For example, your child may not care much about flowers, but your neighbor may prize his flower garden. When your child plays outside, she needs to respect your neighbor's feelings. If he is a close neighbor, ask him to give your family a garden tour. Let him explain how much work it takes to make his garden grow. Remind your child that the flowers in the garden belong to your neighbor, and that she must be careful not to walk on them or pick them.

When you take walks with your child, point out things in the neighborhood that people own and are proud of. Explain that it takes a long time to save up money to buy a car, rent an apartment, or build a house, and that people work hard to keep them looking nice. These explanations should help her understand why we need to respect the property of others.

Brighter Vision Publications · 18 · BV15022 Raising Responsible Kids

Nurturing Community Responsibility

Thinking of Others

Your child is not too young to be caring and supportive of relatives and friends.

There are many ways you can help your child become more aware of the needs of others and do things that make others happy. Here are just a few of them.

- Write thank-you notes and let him add pictures and dictated messages. Send the cards to relatives and friends.
- Let him help make cookies to take to a shut-in friend.
- Show him how to use glue, felt scraps, yarn pieces, pipe cleaners, feathers, or fake fur to turn a smooth stone into a "pet rock" for a relative or a friend who cannot have a real pet.
- Have him make a get-well card or a picture to send to a friend or a relative who is ill or sick.

Community Caring and Sharing

Show your child how caring and sharing can extend to your community.

Use activities such as the ones below to help your child take part in caring for the world around her and the people in it.

- Let her help when you and your neighbors work together to collect trash or clean up brush in the park.
- Involve her in taking extra canned goods or outgrown clothing to a food bank or a homeless shelter.
- Have her accompany you when you do volunteer work.
- Take her to a senior center to drop off wildflowers or to show off her Halloween costume.

Nurturing Community Responsibility

Playtime Rules

Four- and five-year-olds develop a strong sense of fairness when helping make rules.

Your child will be more cooperative in playing with other children at your home if you let him help make the rules for playtime behavior.

Together, decide how many children can come to play at one time, and what should happen if there is a fight over toys or if someone hits or calls names. State your rules positively: "Modeling dough stays at the table. We share the blocks. Keep two steps apart when you climb the slide and hold on with both hands."

Before play starts, review your rules by asking, not telling. Say, "What is our rule about . . . ?" When children are asked to remember and tell, they are more likely to pay attention. Ask them to explain the reason for each rule and thank them for remembering and cooperating.

Stealing

Responsible actions always teach more than words.

Help your child realize that stealing is an irresponsible behavior that hurts others. If you discover that your child has taken something, like a small toy from a toy store, the best thing to do is to remain calm. Explain to him that the toy is the property of the store, and that taking it without paying for it is wrong. Tell him that if everyone took toys without paying for them, the owner wouldn't be able to buy new toys for children like him to buy.

Then take your child back to the store and make him give the toy back. Have him apologize to the owner. Be calm and polite. There is no need for blaming or guilt-producing lectures. Keep the experience a positive one so that your child won't be afraid to accept responsibility for his actions.

Brighter Vision Publications   BV15022 Raising Responsible Kids

Nurturing Community Responsibility

Rules in the Homes of Others

Respect and learn from rules that others follow in their homes.

Before you visit family and friends, make your child aware that rules can be different in other people's homes. Ask your family and friends to clarify their house rules. Make sure your child understands any rules that may be unfamiliar to him, and give him reminders as needed. Tell your child that along with the rules in this home, he still needs to follow your own family rules. If your friends allow their children to run in the house, but you don't allow running in your home, you can still ask your own child to "Please walk." Encourage your child to remember to say "please" and "thank you," whether or not your relatives' children do.

Rules in the Community

Knowing community rules keeps everyone safe.

When you teach your child about respecting the property of others, it's also a good time to introduce the idea of public property. Explain that roads, parks, shopping centers, and sidewalks belong to all of us and are shared by many people of all ages. We need to be sure that everyone can use them easily and safely. Your child needs to know that there are rules in your community that everyone must follow, and that most of these rules are made to help keep people safe in these public areas.

Some rules and safety skills that your child should be aware of include the following.

- Car seat and seat belt laws
- What to do at a stop sign
- What road construction signs mean
- What traffic lights mean
- How to cross streets safely
- Where to put trash in public places
- Laws regulating bikes, skates, and skateboards on sidewalks

Brighter Vision Publications

BV15022 Raising Responsible Kids

Introducing Social Skills

Be An Active Listener

Active listening is an important tool for developing social skills.

Active listeners hear more than just our words. They hear what we are thinking and feeling. They listen to what is behind our words.

Practice active listening with your child. When he is speaking, try to guess what he is thinking and feeling, and ask questions that will help him say more. For instance, you might say, "It sounds like you are really angry with your friend today. Maybe your feelings are hurt. Do you want to tell me about it?" If he looks upset, you might say, "What happened to your happy smile? You look like you want to tell me something. I have time to listen." When you model active listening, your child will tell you more and will learn how he, too, can become an active listener.

Introducing Social Skills

Courage and Honesty

The honesty and courage that your child learns in the home will affect her actions beyond the home.

Accepting responsibility for a mistake takes courage and honesty. These are important social skills to reinforce in your child through positive parental modeling. When you make mistakes, take responsibility for them. Try not to engage in false flattery, white lies, or half-truths in her presence. For example, avoid asking your child to say you're not at home if someone calls whom you don't want to talk to. Let your child know that telling the truth is sometimes a difficult thing to do, but it's the right thing to do.

If your child does something wrong and admits it on her own, take her honesty into consideration. Be gentle but fair about the consequences of her misbehavior, and tell her how proud you are that she had the courage to tell the truth.

Learning About Sharing

Learning to share and take turns is a gradual process.

Your child needs to learn that some toys or materials are things he shares with others. You can force him to take turns, but that's not what you really want. You want him to understand that sharing and taking turns is the right thing to do and that, if the situation were reversed, he would want others to share or take turns with him.

Children gradually learn to share and take turns, and the most important learning begins with your modeling. Let your child see you sharing and taking turns, and tell him that this is what you are doing. As a family, you share pillows on the couch, foods from serving bowls, and drinks from pitchers. You take turns with the newspaper, the toaster, the microwave, the car, the telephone, the computer, and the TV remote control. If you make your child aware of all of the sharing that occurs within your home on a daily basis, he will learn how to begin imitating this behavior.

Brighter Vision Publications

Introducing Social Skills

Sharing Feelings

To share feelings leads to closer conversations with others.

Children who are able to accept and talk about both their "good" and "bad" feelings are demonstrating communication skills that will help them form solid, positive, cooperative relationships.

When they can talk freely about their feelings, fears, ideas, needs, and dreams, children become better able to listen to and empathize with others. This kind of listening and talking is the foundation for getting along well with others.

Practice these skills with your child by taking time each day to share feelings and by modeling good listening behavior for her to imitate and learn.

Positive Social Talk

Positive social language is the cornerstone of good manners.

Family times such as mealtimes offer parents many opportunities to model the positive language that children need to learn in order to be socially skilled. For instance, at mealtimes you may find your child imitating you when you model such phrases as "Thank you," "Please pass the butter," or "Excuse me."

If your child forgets a phrase you have taught him to use when making a request, it's easy to say, "How do we ask for the milk?" Congratulate your child on his good manners and continue to use them yourself.

Introducing Social Skills

Using Descriptive Talk

Descriptive talk is the kind of communication that improves social skills.

Descriptive comments tell others what we really mean or what we really like or dislike. When speaking with your child, use descriptive comments, encouragement, and explanations. Describe what you see her doing and what you feel and think about it. Below are a few examples of how you might do this.

- "You're using a lot of green in that painting. Green is a color that makes me feel peaceful, like when I lie on the grass and look up at the trees."
- "I see that you're making something interesting with the blocks. Can you tell me about it?"
- "I can see that you're angry with your brother. Tell him in words how you feel and what you want."
- "Thank you! It was really thoughtful of you to remember how much I like pine cones and to find one for me on your walk with Grandma."

Tact and Truth

You can help your child learn how to be truthful and tactful at the same time.

Teach your child how to tell the truth without hurting someone else's feelings. If a friend gives her a gift of a book or a toy that she already has, she needs to know how to thank the gift-giver with tact as well as truth. It's a good idea to prepare your child before gifts are given with meaningful things she can say besides "Thank you." For instance, she could say, "I really like this book," or "Thanks, I'm really glad you could come to my party," or "Thanks for being my friend and giving me this present." Stress that giving a gift is a way of showing caring, and that the thought counts more than the gift.

Nurturing Anti-Bias Attitudes

Special Needs Children

Understanding disabilities will help your child make friends with those with special needs.

Teach your child that sometimes special-needs children have special challenges that make it necessary for them to act or do things differently. Explain that some of these children often need special tools such as wheelchairs, neck braces, eyeglasses, or hearing aids to make it easier for them to see, hear, move, or play on their own. Let her know that these tools aren't toys, and that children with special needs depend on them to stay safe.

When you have the opportunity, point out to your child people who have achieved success in spite of disabilities. Be conscious of the way that people with special needs are represented in the books, magazines, and television programs that you share with her. If she attends a school or child-care center, encourage her teachers or caregivers to borrow a wheelchair, walker, or crutches for the children to examine and use. To extend learning at home, put eyeglasses (with the lenses removed) in your child's dress-up box. Teach her about signing and regularly use simple words and phrases in sign, such as "work," "play," "hug," and "I love you."

Brighter Vision Publications

BV15022 Raising Responsible Kids

Nurturing Anti-Bias Attitudes

Homes

There are many kinds of "houses" and all of them are homes.

Help your child understand that people live in various kinds of homes. These dwellings may not all look the same, but they are all homes in which people live. Start by pointing out different kinds of homes in your neighborhood. Do people live in houses of different colors, shapes, sizes, and materials? Do they live in duplexes or in various kinds of apartment houses? What about in condos, mobile homes, or RVs?

Follow up by showing your child pictures of homes found in other parts of the country or the world. Compare the colors, sizes, and shapes of the homes and the materials from which they are made. Talk about fun things you could do if you lived in these homes.

Different Is Interesting

Positive attitudes about differences in others is one of the most important things you can teach.

Today's children will live and work in a world that is fast becoming a global village. They will need to know how to cooperate successfully with people from different backgrounds, cultures, and religions. This is why it is so important for your child to learn positive attitudes about differences in others.

Children are not born with biases and prejudices, but they learn them quickly from what others say or do.

You can combat bias by showing your child that different does not mean better or worse—different is simply different, and quite interesting. Point out simple differences among members of your own family, your friends, and your neighbors. Try not to focus on physical differences only, but on the different ways people work, play, and think. As your child's world expands and he meets different kinds of people, expand your teaching.

Brighter Vision Publications

BVI5022 Raising Responsible Kids

Nurturing Anti-Bias Attitudes

Foods

Tasting a variety of breads introduces your child to differences in foods.

Whenever possible, include foods from other regions and countries in your family meals. You might want to start by introducing various kinds of breads. Everyone, all over the world, eats bread of some kind. Help your child come to understand that although the breads may be different in some ways, they are all breads that people need and like to eat.

Purchase different kinds of breads for your family, one at a time, to eat along with what you usually buy. Try pita breads, French or Italian breads, tortillas, fry bread, cornbread, rye bread, and so forth. Talk about the tastes and textures of each bread. Also, use a map or a globe to show your child the countries in which the breads originated. Continue by gradually including new kinds of fruits or vegetables in your family meals.

Broadening Horizons

Teach your child about the differences and similarities among various cultures.

With your child, look for library picture books about children of other cultures. Read about children with different backgrounds in our own country, not just in other lands. When looking for books about difference, bias, and prejudice, be sure to include Dr. Seuss's *The Sneetches and Other Stories*. These stories deal with anti-bias issues using situations that children can relate to, such as being excluded from games and parties, or being afraid of someone until meeting them and finding out what they're like. The inventive language engages young children while broadening their awareness.

Also, collect magazine pictures of children and adults from different cultures who show a variety of expressions such as surprise, fear, joy, anger, sadness, and excitement. Cut out the pictures, mount them on cardboard or posterboard, and cover them with clear self-stick paper. Use the pictures to talk with your child about feelings. Help her to understand that all people have the same kinds of feelings, no matter what their age or appearance.

Nurturing Anti-Bias Attitudes

Gender Traps

Let your child's potential, and not his gender, guide your activity choices.

Make sure you offer all kinds of activities, toys, and books to your child, regardless of gender. Check how you've done so far by making a quick and honest inventory of the kinds of toys, books, and activities you have in your home. Do you have dolls (besides action figures) for a boy to play with? Does a girl have a selection of cars and trucks? Does your child play with blocks and other construction materials regardless of gender?

In what sorts of activities do you encourage your child's participation? Is a boy encouraged to help make cookies, and is a girl given simple tools to experiment with? What kinds of children's books do you have? Make any changes or additions needed to help your child feel that boys and girls have equal potential and talents.

Correcting Misconceptions

Speak out whenever you hear a hurtful or untrue comment to help your child avoid bias and prejudice.

One of the most important things you can do to combat bias and prejudice is to immediately correct any misconceptions your child expresses about other children or adults who appear different in some way. ("His nose is too big." "Her eyes are funny looking." "Girls can't drive trucks." "Boys can't play house." "Old people are no fun." "Poor people like junk and are always dirty.")

If you hear such a remark, whether it comes from your child or a friend, speak up calmly, stating that you do not approve of what was said and explaining that the remark is either hurtful or untrue. If appropriate, ask questions to find out the reason for the remark, then correct the misconception. Encourage a healthy attitude toward differences by answering your child's questions honestly and fostering pride, not superiority. When you say nothing, you are giving silent approval. This hurts your child and others. It will foster bias and prejudice and impede the fostering of cooperation.

Brighter Vision Publications   BV15022 Raising Responsible Kids

Cultivating Environmental Awareness

Environmental Awareness

Children need to understand their role in the environment.

Young children can easily learn that they are a part of the natural world and that their actions have an impact on the environment. But before they can feel any responsibility to the environment, they need to become aware that plants, animals, and people all depend on each other, and that all things in nature work together.

Talk about how every living plant or animal depends on other plants and animals to survive. People depend on animals for food and companionship, and on plants for food and clean air.

Some animals depend on people to give them food, some animals eat other animals for food, and some animals depend on plants for food and shelter. Plants are affected by the actions of people and animals.

Plants and animals die and make the soil rich for new plants to grow. Soil nourishes seeds and keeps them warm and moist enough to grow into plants.

When we teach children about nature, we are teaching them the concept of interdependence. Learning about interdependence nurtures responsibility. There are many books about the environment at your local library. One excellent resource is Edward Duensing's *Talking to Fireflies, Shrinking the Moon: A Parent's Guide to Nature Activities.*

Cultivating Environmental Awareness

Trees

Inexpensive packages of tree seedlings can be ordered from the National Arbor Day Foundation.*

Go on a tree hunt with your child around your home to find some of the objects that are made from or use wood products. Then, take a walk in your neighborhood and look at the trees and shrubbery. With the help of books, see if you can identify the names of the trees you find.

Let your child "adopt" a mature tree that is growing nearby, grow a seedling in a large planter, or help him plant a young tree seedling in your yard. If your child has adopted a mature tree, he will enjoy visiting his tree every season to notice and document its changes. Encourage him to examine what is found under the tree, make leaf or bark rubbings, name the tree, talk to it, sing to it, sit under it to think or read, have a snack or a picnic under it, or lie under it to look at the sky. If the tree is on your property, perhaps he'll want to hang a wind chime, bird feeder, or tire swing from its branches. When you visit the tree with your child, discuss the many ways trees help us.

- They protect us from sun or wind.
- They help hold the soil so it doesn't wash away.
- They are home to many animals.
- They provide beauty in all seasons.
- They provide us with fuel for fires.
- They give us flowers, fruits, and nuts.
- They provide us with wood for making houses, toys, furniture, and paper.
- They create many kinds of jobs, including forest rangers, carvers, carpenters, printers, loggers, tree trimmers, landscapers, and toy or furniture makers.
- They "breathe" carbon dioxide and "exhale" oxygen, freshening the air.

*211 N. 12th St., Lincoln, NE 68508

Gardening

Maintaining a garden can be a fun and rewarding family challenge.

If you don't have the space or sun for a small vegetable garden, try making a container garden with your child. With a little creativity, you can turn a balcony, a porch, or a windowsill into a garden space. Buckets, barrels, flower pots, window boxes, hanging planters, plastic dishpans, and plastic tubs are just a few of the many containers that you can use to grow fresh flowers, vegetables, and herbs.

Plan your garden together  and let your child help choose what you grow. Try to vary your planting so that you can enjoy a long growing season. Put your child in charge of watering and weeding the plants. As the plants grow, discuss their characteristics with your child. Point out that often the flowers become the food to be harvested. When a vegetable or herb is ready to harvest, let your child help prepare it as part of a family meal.

Cultivating Environmental Awareness

Recycle

Follow up discussions about recycling with reminders to help prevent littering.

Explain to your child that we throw away a lot of trash, and that one way to throw less away is to use it again. Let your child help you sort through your trash to find recyclables. See if she can think of new ways to reuse some of these objects. Show her the recycling bins in or near your home and have her help you prepare your recyclables for storage by breaking down boxes and washing bottles and cans. Let her watch for the garbage or recycling truck, and see how the items are carried away.

Here are a few additional recycling ideas to practice with your child.

- Use newspaper, brown paper grocery bags, and magazines for art creations.
- Find places to take outgrown clothing and toys, so that others can use them.
- Use fabric remnants to make stuffed toys or pillows.
- Use berry baskets to store small toys.
- Take used magazines to a homeless shelter or to the school's art station.

Conserving Water

Teach your child how important it is to conserve water.

There are many things that your child can do to help conserve water. Teach him how to turn off the faucet while he brushes his teeth or soaps his hands, and to turn it back on only when he's ready to rinse. Keep a pitcher of water in the refrigerator so that he doesn't have to run the tap to get the water cold. Give him short showers instead of tub baths when needed.

Reinforce the importance of conserving water by not letting the faucet run with this experiment. Set a plastic tub inside your sink to catch the water as he washes his hands. Then give your child measuring cups to help you discover how much water he used. You may be surprised at how quickly the tub gets filled.

Brighter Vision Publications